Alexey Vesnin

HyperSphere Whitepaper

09 Oct 2019

Preface

Speaking ahead, a HyperSphere is a huge SDK and to describe it even briefly in less than 100 pages is an impossible task, so there will be two fundamental documents about this project. The one you're starting to read now – the whitepaper – will give you a full overview, so you will have a decent idea about what it is and what it consists of. The second one – it was the first whitepaper I was starting to write – it became a book, so there will be a very deep explanation, real-life case review and all the side notes will be added. It's more than 500 pages, so let it fulfill it's purpose later, as it will be published. All the new ideas, algorithms, and other things are the intellectual property of Alexey Vesnin as the author of this book, all the other stuff that existed before 9th of October 2019 – it belongs to its authors.

Introduction

Today we have quite many blockchain projects, consensus algorithms, and tied ecosystems, so why do I make another one? The answer is short: we don't need just another one system, we need a system so flexible, so it's able to become the one sole system for a real-world tasks. And we don't see such a system efficiently working in a real-life right now: not in a laboratory environment or a regulated sandbox – in the very real world, right behind the corner of the street you're living in. At first we will take a look at the history of the project's idea evolution, so it will make many things clear afterwards in the meaning of automatically answering the question "why this is made exactly that way?", next we will take an overview of all the parts of the project and will see a roadmap for project implementation and integration. To understand even the mathematical definitions mentioned in this book you're not required to have special math skills, all the deep mathematics will be presented in a book.

A history of HyperSphere

The project has been started in late 2011 as a set of patches for Tor and these patches were sent to their support team email address, but they were neither accepted, nor declined – and speaking forward: the functional abilities I've sent were not implemented till today. So I decided to start my fork of Tor, initially compatible with the original network. Time has passed, more patches were made and I've started to finalize a router box with privacy built-in and containing my version of Tor, a Raspberry Pi B+ was an initial platform, so not so many features onboard. Lately in 12th of June 2012, I caught a traffic intrusions and filtering without any legal grounds from my home ISP, so I've made a public lecture about how to defend yourself in Internet in my mother-city, and it was a crystallization point: a community has started to grow up and I've made some more lectures, from time to time some different people came to me with their very real and practical cases – it was more than 100 really different cases. No correlation based on gender, age, area of interest or type of online and offline activity – the only thing in common that internet access was not just filtered, but an active intrusions were performed from the ISP side. So I helped to solve all these cases and has got a wide representation of this real-world problem and – as a logical outcome – it was a self-defense package for every type of case included in my solution. After that, I renamed the project from its initial name "netsafe" to "Project A.R.I.A.D.N.E." which was for Advanced Routing Interconnect Accelerator for Distributed Network Experience, because it has Tor, I2P and basic mesh networks on board. Adding more components for self-defense, I've met a blockchain-based solution. I was keeping my eye on the blockchain industry development just out of my curiosity, and now it was a good time to test it in a real field test. First ones were Namecoin and Emercoin EmerDNS and EmerSSL, so – things have started to become more and more complex at least by the reason of having to run two separate blockchain nodes of each chain, which was not so efficient from the side of resource management at least. And at the same time, it was multiple attempts to elaborate blockchain and smart contracts in different real world tasks, including privacy protection. The very idea of a smart contract was brilliant for me since that time and I tried to apply it to a real problem I have had myself that time and for my project. So I've started to experiment with Ethereum and similar systems after that time – and I was quite disappointed: smart contract virtual machines were either a sphere in a physical vacuum where you can not interact with an outside world almost at all, or a security hole in a box – it looks more like a blockchain integration SDK without any attempt to make an execution context separation for two different smart contracts and because of that it is totally unacceptable too. Looking at the projects which were integrated inside a web browser, I've found the one named Perspectives Project and I loved the idea and has helped them in reviving their firefox add-on code to work again on a new browser version. Looking at the code I could not resist thinking that actually at least half of the functions could be executed in a truly decentralized way with a great amplification of a protection quality. So it could be a smart contract and a distributed application(aka DApp) – and a blockchain seemed to be a perfect interconnect for it. But which one? Neither Namecoin nor Emercoin does not have smart contracts or distributed applications, so – should I add a third one? Should I propose a functionality addition for my particular service task as a C++ patch, but to which one of them? And here I've started to learn deeper about smart contracts and DApps from an architectural point of view – and the only solution was the hardest one to implement: I had to start my blockchain with a smart contract and DApps containers that are actually fitting real-world tasks. And looking at Solidity, NodeJS and another solutions for the parts mentioned, I've made long research and found that the real logical solution is using PHP7 for both, I will explain it later as I will describe the active containers. After a review, I've noticed that modern smart contract demands and DApps will also fit quite well in this implementation, so I was not making any artificial borders for implementing fintech, DeFi and all the other stuff on a platform – they are a real-world tasks too, so let people be able to solve them as well in a single ecosystem and not have such a problem as running multiple networks' nodes as I had myself at the beginning. This approach has added some handy features to the HyperSphere – a person can solve the problem better if the problem was this very person's real problem in the past. So that's why you won't find a fintech or DeFi or even the blockchain-related focus on this document: the HyperSphere is about to help real people solve real problems they encounter and a blockchain is neither a purpose, nor an ideology in this project – it's an important component, no more.

HyperSphere structure

In its current state, the project consists of the parts listed:
- Linux distribution, including OpenWRT and Android parts
- Blockchain backbone
- Networking backbone
- Active containers
- Application containers

Each component will be described in more details, but to prevent questions about the wallet software and other stuff related: a wallet exists to fulfill its purpose and just for that. For all the rest of the functions, we do have a wide and handy API to build an integration you want. We're not pre-building anything for you, we're giving you a tool to do so, metaphorically speaking.

Linux distribution

As the project began to manifest, even on a netsafe stage, we have faced some ubiquitous but not less painful problem – compatibility. Different Linux distributions have had a different libraries in their repositories, and sometimes the difference was so big, that it was literally breaking the build and it was a snowball becoming an avalanche as it rolled out. Especially on ARM single-board computers, we've often seen a basic BSP = Board Support Package - from a chip manufacturer tuned up to be able to physically run some common software fetched out of Debian or Ubuntu binary repositories, and the software itself was quite old and slow. At the same time in a git trunk of Linux kernel it was like an explosion of board support range, but you have to run the kernel version 3.xxx which was old enough to be attacked, which is totally unacceptable when we are about to defend ourselves using this setup or to perform some coin transactions on it.

At first, I was sticking to Debian as a basement for a setup, because it was the distribution that caused me minimal problems in manual kernel upgrade. But other matters has forced me to make a separate distribution, like the inability to have two library versions on one system at the same time. And having started a distribution, I've set some strict rules behind its architecture:
1. *The OS distribution has to be a core*. Not everything. Active containers and Application containers can solve the things up seamlessly and secure, the Qubes OS project has proven it well including a time-proof.
2. *The package system has to be flexible*. I've started to upgrade APT system to add two missing features that are required anyway, but they are crucial when you're working with single board computers or IoT or embedded systems: a flavor – is it a static or a dynamic version, and a CPUArch – yes, you can run i386 or i686 code on the latest Core i9, but will it work as fast as it supposed to? It's a common problem: you're buying decent hardware as an upgrade and you're expecting a performance increase respectively to the hardware difference, but experience reveals just a simple small increase of the numbers.
3. *Don't run anything you do not need*.
4. *In a package building system, it has to be full cascaded testing*. Yes, it sounds obvious, but the building system has to be not just a building system – it has to be a proper cascaded testing system. Why cascading all the tests? If you have recompiled a new version of the library, let's say its OpenSSL – its tests will pass just fine and well, but another software can have unexpected problems popping out of the holes. So – if the library is compiled and it's a new version – we're hitting two targets at once. First of all, we're ensuring that it won't break other packets, because we will deploy a new version only after the full success of all the underlying test tree. Second benefit, but only by an order of mentioning, underlying packages will be rebuilt if their tests are not passing successfully, so we will push not just a new library, but all the necessary updates for a depending packages, and we will push only ones we do really need to rebuild: tests are preserved after a build for this exact purpose, so they will try to pull out a new shared library and will initially try to work with a new library so as the package they're related to.

Working with Linux distribution I was able to adapt the packets for ARM chips, so the next logical outcome was OpenWRT – after re-merging with project LeDe that was a fork of the original old OpenWRT there was still an old kernel and packet versions. After some tests I was able to have up to 20% performance increase on a SOHO router that costs like 50 USD – so on the top models, there can be a very impressive result.

And if some who knows me in person is reading this right now, a question will be – why not FreeBSD? Yes, I've spent a lot of time working with that exact OS and even as a teacher about that OS. Sadly, the ARM board support was so narrow in FreeBSD at the time of making this decision, so it was no choice.

Final releases and even release candidates are used in our package repository to provide up-to-date but stable infrastructure, except for a kernel and libraries like OpenSSL – stable releases are used as well as master/trunk ones with the pull requests that are really fixing things, not breaking the build but re not merged in yet. We're using latest kernel of the same version on all hardware platforms with one single exception – some exotic ARM CPU's or SoC's do have problems with a new versions from time to time, so we're not breaking the things by enforcing the upgrades – this kind of situation is a very rare one nowadays, and I hope someday it will be a history totally. As a building system we're using Jenkins CI with custom scripts and plugins, so this tool allows us to have the process as fine-grained, as we need it.

Active containers

As I have mentioned above, we do have smart contracts and DApps and both of them are using PHP7 as their language of implementation. So it's obvious, that we have to implement a container for running it. And here we have some pros and cons that we have to take into account to make the system fitting the real-world. First question here – why are we even speaking about such a thing as a container for a smart contract? All the rest of the industry do use a virtual machine for them – and here is the root of the problem. In a mobile world, the solution was introduced more than a decade ago, but it needs to be evolved to apply it to a blockchain.

The solution is called a capability list, or "caps". If you will try to run embedded – as it said – Ethereum node in a router on OpenWRT – trust me, you will surprise yourself because you'll be swearing that hard that you could not imagine before in most of the cases. And – generally – it's not even a node code problem – it's just too tough for an embedded device: yes, it can run itself and even do something, but it will consume so many resources than for the rest of the device's functionality there will be almost nothing left. And this very "rest of functionality" is the thing that ais solving the task the device is made for, so – if you need to check the balance of the wallet to verify the payment status – why do you need to run a smart contract on a device? Run a lightweight node, so you will be able to just check a balance and a transaction log to do your job – and waste no drop of any kind of resource that you're do not need at all in that particular case? Use your device's resources to solve your real-world problem with that device!

If your device is a mobile one – you can make it consisting of two parts, two SoC's – one is a low-power slow main one with a light node, but if you'll need to run a smart contract on a very rare occasion – you can fire-up the second more powerful SoC as a USB slave device in a gadget mode, perform the calculations – and put it back offline. The battery power consumption will be improved greatly here. But will it require some new interfaces to be designed, e.t.c…? Certainly not – it has been already done: Linux kernel has full support for a gadget mode with networking support, JSON-RPC is a normal thing in any wallet and PHP has got a networking PHP-FPM interface for many years.

Another capability benefit is an ability to run a different type of smart contracts that do need to access a real world outside the container. Maybe you will need to read a pulse sensor, or a temperature sensor, or get some data from NFC interaction that are signed by the private key on a remote device? It's normal! So you can select which kind of smart contracts you're generally allowing, and – if you need to use some specific smart contract, like the check-in one which needs your geolocation – you can make an exception for a specific smart contract as well. It's like an SELinux or AppArmor system, but for a smart contract.

Okay, we have a smart contract subject covered, but what about the DApps? The answer is in another question – what is the difference between a DApp and a smart contract?

I am generally determining two types of DApps: resident smart-contract-like ones and a decentralized desktop application(which needs GUI, device interaction e.t.c.). First ones can be executed exactly like smart contracts with the mechanism described above, they will just have an additional API's available for them. The second ones are fully-featured applications and they do need a separate container type, which is an Application container.

For an application of the first type, there's also an isolated network on pub/sub and p2p transport is available, but only an instances of this application are inside this network to prevent DDoS and another types of abuse. Also, there is an ability to bridge pub/sub transports of this type of networks if this is allowed by both applications' capabilities. So, to finish the picture – any application can publish its API endpoint for a local usage, which can be extremely useful when using API like Nvidia CUDA in connection with an application running inside an Application container.

One of the most demanding types of the DApps is a truly distributed oracle – only with HyperSphere you can write it on PHP, push the source code into the system and it will be an ability to use and run it everywhere in a system without any custom software installation or custom node compilation like in Ethereum. And because of the API of the system, you can offer people to run your oracle to power up the smart contracts directly connected to the real world: a contract can be triggered if a person is at the specific location, for example.

Taking a deeper look into this kind of container we can see that a modern APIs like OpenCL and Nvidia CUDA can be easily elaborated using Zend's versatile binding API without any harm to either a privacy nor to the confidentiality. A scientific initiative like Folding at home can achieve a magnitude greater results if they will elaborate the API's regardless of the particular device and installation – and it will be a truly decentralized experience.

One more interesting content and app integration idea is an IVR = Interactive Voice Response, so you will be able to talk with your application or a website natively and all your data will be processed locally unless you will indicate your decision to make it elsewhere. We're actually on an eve of a new technological revolution and all we're desperately missing now is a single ecosystem to make it all work together.

Making a summary: there're a lot of tasks nowadays that can be and should be decentralized, the only problem is that we do have an incapable system to do so. Until now.

Application containers

In an opposition to the active containers, which are a PHP7 containers insulated as a separate process, this type of container has a significant difference. First of all, if this is a fully-featured application – it handles not just a GUI and sensitive interaction with a user like audio and video streams, it handles data outside itself. So the data can be opened from a storage media and saved to it, and this fact changes the security model completely. Inventing the wheel is not a method in privacy, so we're expanding the approach used in the Qubes OS project: an isolation is made not on a process level, but at least on a process tree one. We do have a different insulation types for application containers: it's either a Docker container or a separate VM with its dedicated kernel running. Why we not just adopt the approach of virtualizing pools of applications or a separate ones? The answer is a resource cost: it's a way faster and costs less to just separate the application inside a Docker container rather than rising a full machine for it. This difference can be not a significant one on a powerful systems or even on a regular desktop PC performing some daily task, but if we will look at IoT and embedded world – this overhead can be not just a performance issue, but a blocker because the target system will not have the desired amount of RAM or CPU to run everything it needs to perform its task. So here we're giving full freedom to the end-user or a solution developer to set the security points across the architectural map of their solution. Yes, you can run inside a VM a program that needs just a Docker container, but not vice versa. And the application origins can be as it fits: it can be a PHP7 DApp, or it can be a regular desktop application like a web browser.

Using a flexible virtualization and Docker link gives us an ability to use Application container in one interesting way as well – it can be a VPS which can be rented by the network users, so people can monetize their idle hardware resources efficiently, developers can obtain a testing container on the desired hardware type to make a native tests and compilation, it's just a distributed hosting platform. Here I must make a strong remark about the data privacy: containers and virtual machines are as unsafe and not private, as on the regular hosting providers. This means that the data could be read, copied and tampered by the hosting party with the same difficulty level, as it can be done in a centralized hosting provider company. So there was, there are and there will be the tasks – like the ones who are working with sensitive data – that you still have to solve in an old way, but the fog computing is literally at your hand now. And also take into account one small but significant fact: hosting market due to its centralized nature has got some price level coordination just because of its nature, it can't be cheap because of too many middle man involved – but what will be, if we will be paid directly to the people who will provide their spare resources? The market will be truly free and the price drop is expected to the reasonable levels.

Also if we will proceed in digging deeper into the matter of the problem – some clone of a Dockerfile can be provided for an application container, especially for the one we have as a fully virtualized one. This brings us a more transparent market for pre-built solutions. Yes, I'm not talking about re-inventing a docker repository – only to make it more transparent. For example: you're starting your docker container from an Ubuntu LTS image… Wait a minute – why can't you provide a checksum for that image in the same instruction? Or a public key checksum? So – speaking more directly – you can not control the consistency or content of the image you're starting from! OK, you may add a way to control the checksum of the custom packages you're installing further – but a start? What if it was modified? Or what if it is containing a backdoor? Or – let us raise the full question – what is under the hood? A Sol.EXE, maybe – in a next update? And about a solitary executable – it's not a joke: it was demonstrated on a BlackHat that mangling signatures you can put it instead of the executable file during update – dig some YouTube!

Network backbone

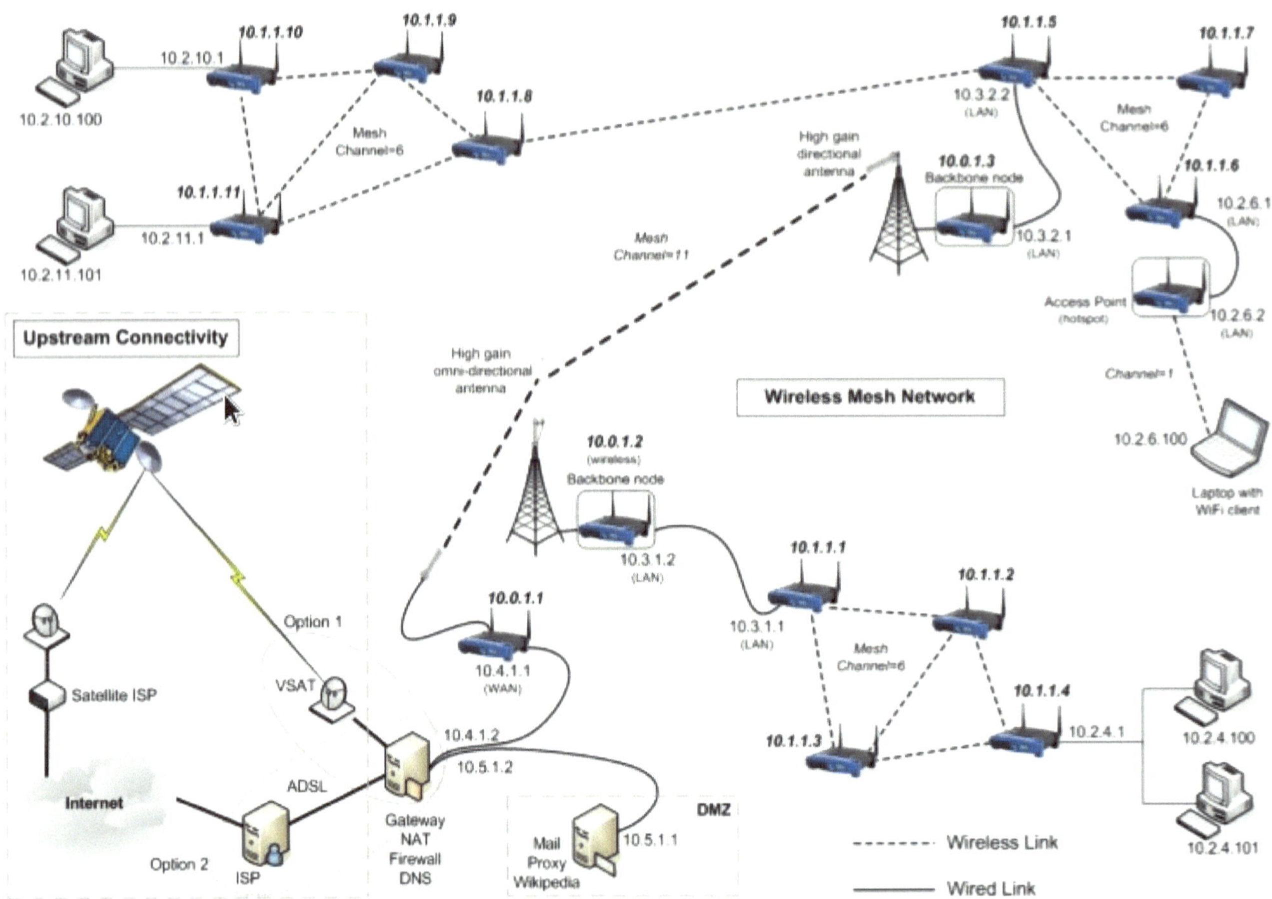

Picture by David Johnson, Karel Matthee, Dare Sokoya, Lawrence Mboweni, Ajay Makan, and Henk Kotze (Wireless Africa, Meraka Institute, South Africa) [CC BY-SA 2.5]

The project has started from a secure router and definitely it's a heart of the system. You can not have a reliable network of any type – blockchain, LAN, VPN, anything – if your channels are easily disrupted or overloaded or cost too much to be affordable for your end-users. That's how the network layer here is working – we're making a hybrid stack with a unified API to utilize OTT(On The Top – a mode when something is running on a base of another thing, like Tor is running over the Internet) and standalone mode at the same time. Why it's so important nowadays – let's take a look.

As the network has started to grow – a throughput requirement has grown much faster than a number of users connected to the Internet, so in the first days we have had a long-range and that situation has named the problem – a last-mile problem. An ISP can have a decent connection to the outside world, but every user is not connected to this exit directly, like in one switch – so we have a daisy-chaining of the links and interconnects from the very outbound exit to the end user's device, and the slowest link makes a limit here. So – how this dial-up era problem is related to us today? We still have a case, when an ISP will not go to someplace because it's too expensive, or – as some kind of the opposite – the site is connected, but the link is loaded too high most of the times, so overall speed is poor because of that. What's the solution?

One of the most interesting solutions is a mesh network that we are using. To briefly describe the benefit of using mesh networks let us give a clear definition of the mesh network: it's a self-organizing network with dynamic topology and real-time link construction. How can it be of service? Let's take a look at the usual cases we do have nowadays every day and every one of us.

Let us take a look at torrents: your neighbor next flat to you has got a piece of the file you're downloading right now. Yes, the tracker will connect you both with each other – but how? You will be contacting your neighbor through the ISP infrastructure – from your PC to the router, to its router and to the BRAS – the device that makes a gateway for local users to reach an outer world, a Broadband Remote Access Server. And your neighbor will send you the packets in the same manner – but why should you both make not a double load on the last mile infrastructure because of the fact that each of his packets is going to the BRAS and then it comes back to you in the same way, why can't you just use a Wi-Fi through the wall to make a direct transfer not making a single bit of load to the last mile at all? The core of the problem is that the external IP addresses are given to you both by the ISP, and nobody knows that you two are living next door to each other. In mesh networks the address is derived from your public key – and this uniqueness can be easily ensured by the blockchain registry – and yes, the tracker will still give you an external address of your neighbor just because it can not see his other details, but next step the mesh routing is coming to play: it will determine that you do have a direct link and will utilize it automatically, no configuration required for this to happen. And not just both of you will have a decent speed, but also no parasitic load will be done on the last mile ISP infrastructure, so if another user will need to make a distant long-reaching query to the server in another country, it will have a free channel with a proper bandwidth.

Not just a torrent can be mended with mesh networks, but a very useful service like CDN = Content Delivery Network. The conception of CDN is a distributed cache at its heart, i.e. if you have a static piece of data that is not changing, you can put it on the servers near the end-users and they will get it from there rather than using your server. The problem is not just the fact that in some countries CDN's are being hunted by authorities like Google Cache servers in Russia – the demand is still too high even for modern data transfer channels. But – wait a minute – there're a lot of JavaScript frameworks like jQuery and things like Google Fonts, Google Analytics, Yandex Metrika are relatively small and used on most of the sites – why do we still need to query a remote server for it? Open your WiFi capable device at home and take a look at the network list. In most of the cases you will have at least 5-7 of the neighbor networks with a fast speed around and there're also some people who are using websites frequently as well – so, if we will check the digital signature using a blockchain we do already have locally – why can't we just grab these pieces from the neighbor devices? Data integrity won't be lost because of the signing and the overall speed of the websites will be a magnitude higher than it's now – and still the same, without any parasitic load on the last mile.

Another benefit of the mesh networks is that they're reorganizing their topology constantly, so – you can walk on the street with your mesh-enabled gadget and you need to check the mail, for example. If you're in a foreign country – it can be expensive due to the roaming fees, and it can be a cell base station overload which will make your day a nightmare – but what if on this street a person lives who has an unlimited internet access? Through a blockchain mechanism this person can set up the ability to give it's spare or unused bandwidth to the ones who need it, and you will be able to transfer some coins automatically to this person to get an access to the Internet to check your mail? The benefit is triple here: a cellular ISP has his base station loaded with lower requests, you haven't overpaid for traffic and that person can earn coins to reduce some bills, like the ISP ones? How many people do have their home routers online constantly, even when they're not at home? Why don't their devices make them some coins, especially from a regular automatic airdrop?

Will it kill the ISP's? Will it hurt their business? No. On the contrary – it will expand it because we can not make a global single mesh, we will need their infrastructure of cables as a backbone, so their services will be in the same demand. And for ISP it's a really good opportunity to expand its last-mile with mesh networks without making an expensive cable extension works: the ISP can put its services like IP TV, video on demand, VoIP and others into the global system and make it available as widely as possible to the maximal audience without a single penny spent on marketing. Sounds good, isn't it?

To implement it technically we're using a multi-layered mesh bridging to avoid the flood fill problem and as a basement we're using a modified versions of B.A.T.M.A.N for OSI Layer 2 and Yggdrasil and cjDNS for OSI Layer 3, routing protocols and schematics will be disclosed in details in a book – sadly, it can't be described in 10 pages…

Last, but not less significant practical application for mesh networks is a disaster recovery and catastrophic emergencies scenario, when the landlines are damaged or destroyed – mesh networks are utilizing any channel available, so even in such a situation it will automatically build a new topology in tenths of seconds, so end-users will have an ability to call for help or transmit an important message.

But when we're about to deploy a mesh network – regardless of its type – we have to make a descriptor for every node that is participating the network, and – doing that – we will have to maintain a descriptor repository so we will be able to deflect false packets. This was solved as a descriptor problem – see down strings, the solution will be described as it will be clear about how it works. For now, we will make a statement that it's an external daemon process tat maintains the registry.

Digging deeper, we will reveal the broadcast and multicast packets problem. The mesh networks – from a structural level – are supposed to be a single-ranked ones, so we have to re-transmit all the broadcasts and multicasts across all the network members. However, the only useful application for this kind of packets is a multicast service announcements – but we do have a blockchain, so all we have to do is to standardize the listening ports for any service and make it available by default on every node. So the casts are efficiently stripped out on both sending and receiving sides – to prevent the attacks on mesh segments. OSI Level 2 broadcasts from Yggdrasil and cjDNS are all we need to maintain the mesh network consistency.

Another important moment is that we will delay the inter-segment links because a mobile device walking around will be able to pick multiple segments once, but later it will lose a link to at least one of them. So we're using a connectivity points system to determine the permanency of the link: each time the device hits the segment as available, it gains a score reduced by the number of checkup iterations, so it will reach a threshold value in a non-linear mode slower, like this:

$$S = \frac{X + c}{X + c + 1}$$

Where we have:
- X is previous iteration value. 0 if it's a first one
- c is a number of connections for another segment
- S is the new X for a next evaluation

This evaluation is made from both sides, so you will have a stable result in a relatively short time with a proper threshold – and we will not have a problem of too frequent segment reconfiguration. However, this rule is not applied to the lightweight state machines of blockchain – even in 10-30 seconds on a modern Wi-Fi or Lo-Ra speeds it's more than enough time to exchange the saving points. However, to make an inter-segment bridge it takes much longer time for a model to settle in – so we can be ensured in two most frequent network topology scenarios to behave properly:

- If it's _a single-touch_ with a mobile router in a bag of a walking person – the save points will be transmitted to protect the integrity of a blockchain.
- If it's _a long-term_ connection, it will be elaborated properly and will bridge two segments in the shortest way by the means of network hops count.

The question here is will it have to be a mutual acceptance from both segments at the same time? The answer is no – because all the IP addresses are derived from a public keys that were announced beforehand, so the network will know if it's capable of handling the valid packet and will have enough knowledge to drop forged ones for sure. And – in time – for a router being connected to two segments simultaneously for some time – it will be accepted as a bridge by both segments.

Another important question that was found and is still under research a many years ago – how many nodes can be in a single mesh segment at the same time? With a basic settings as soon as we're hitting the OSI Level 3 – it's like some hundreds, 200 or 300 nodes, no more. Broadcast traffic and other factors are killing it's a benefit to the ground. If the broadcasts are filtered out – it's arising to the 1000, but no more. These numbers are real because of the deep digging into the nature of the channels used in the tests. A Wi-Fi – even with the MU-MIMO we do have a speed reduction with the number of clients increasing in a spot. So – using a higher band like 5GHz we will actually have no more than 300-500 devices in a close segment or a vicinity, and an inter-segment links can be easily handled by a 2.4GHz links even if there are no wired ones.

That's actually why the old times' approach of using a switch for a porch or a flat group is on the rise again – it can be utilized well and it is working on a global scale. The problem of these synthetic tests is that only a 2.4GHz Wi-Fi was used and this channel alone. At the time of that tests a LoRa WAN modules were not so widely accessible and slow as hell both – so it's a decent result for that time. But now we can use a much more wider set of interfaces, including different LoRa ones to make a network considerable fast and reliable.

The global purpose of the network backbone is to give back to the Internet it's literal meaning: Inter Networking – fast, free and untampered.

Blockchain backbone

So as we have a brief overview of the functional parts, let us proceed with the thing that brings it all together as one solution – the blockchain. The blockchain as we know it today was invented in the early 1990s, and because of the Bitcoin appearance on the stage – it was a lot of projects, integrations, and time-proven cases. Nothing stays the same, and it has to evolve to survive, so the blockchain does. Let us proceed from the very basic terms to represent the full idea of our improved blockchain subsystem.

First of all, let's speak about the consensus algorithm – there were Proof-of-Work and Proof-of-Stake at the very beginning, but now we do have a lot of logical ones. In my opinion the only algorithm that can be trusted is a pure computational one because there is no potential logical clashes or bombs and 2 plus 2 is always a four – in any condition, on any hardware platform. So a PoW was chosen as a basement for a consensus, because it grants you a distributed and truly equal ability for every node to produce a block. However, looking at Bitcoin and Ethereum, we do see a difficulty avalanche problem, and a sharding is totally not a solution here – sharding splits the problem to the smaller merely-connected parts, not solving it and makes things a way more complicated, like a get block request when you will be forced to query all the shards now. Also looking at Ethereum mining pools producing empty blocks just because it's faster – we can spot the problem: the classical PoW procedures are needed to be evolved.

On the other hand, PoS is capable of producing blocks relatively fast and it has no difficulty problem. However, it's complicated to re-elect the signing nodes and in DPoS = Delegated PoS – it's impossible to re-elect the signing quorum on the fly: to make different votes/delegations you still need the blockchain working, and if it's not – the network is stale.

Also, starting with Dash crypto coin, we have a masternode term which means that a node can perform additional tasks with a safety deposit previously locked to provide a byzantine problem tolerance. After that time, a PIVX coin has made a masternode as we used to see it now in a numerous altcoins produced from it, so the thesis is time-proven also. The safety deposit is locked not just to provide insurance so the system can punish in coins the false or misbehaving node – it's also providing a scarcity of resources that is essential for a mining process on a coin supply level.

So what solution do I propose? It's a hybrid system that consists of the compartments listed below, the list numbering is an order of the block processing:
1. *Network quorum.* A transaction is signed by the issuer's private key and is pushed into the network in a decentralized way: a node interacts not with the quorum generally, but with its neighbors as well – it's like a snowflake with a broadcasting node in the middle
2. *Mempool.* A standard de facto for a modern blockchain systems. And a lot of stale conditions were caused by its overflow, so – as we will have it's contents from step 1 propagated, we're proceeding to step 3. At this step all sanity checks are provided, like if it's a coin transfer – is there enough balance to do so? If any sanity check is failing here – the transaction is dropped out of the pool, notifying the neighbor nodes and the consensus to check for themselves and to do the same.
3. *MemDB.* PoS controlled by automatically re-electable pool of masternodes and adding its oldest contents into the MemDB chain. It's a very mathematically important fact that the list of transactions coming to the block is finalized now. This kind of helper structure ensures us from mempool overflow and reduces the resource costs of running a node drastically – as the transaction came into the MemDB, it is removed from a mempool, so the blockchain node can free the memory used to store it safely. And the get block logic is intact – because it's not final block storage, you're still querying the blockvortex for blocks, and memdb is queried by getting cache query, so as the mempool – it will return an additional boolean part in result – where is the block?
4. *Blockvortex.* Yes, it's not a chain any more – it's a 3D structure, how it works it will be explained later. A finalized by contents on step 3 block is inserted into the slot in the structure and mined by PoW miners, then the mined block is signed by elected masternodes – and we do have a classical PoW/PoS here. After that happened – a block in memdb is marked as mined and the transactions are beginning to mature as usual in blockchains nowadays. Yes, I've forgot to mention – we have just mathematically killed the classical 51% attack on a PoW blockchain consensus here: even if somebody will try and hypothetically succeed in making 51% PoW

attack – the false data will not be found in memdb so the forged block will be marked as invalid just by making a list to list comparison which has a nearly-zero resource cost, so even a smartwatch or a small IoT device could not be tricked.

5. *State machines.* We do have a checkpoint mechanism, but to maintain it as we are doing it today, we have to make a binary upgrade, because the checksum and block reference is hardcoded into the source code. State machines are the blockchains also, but with a tiny block with the necessary information. It's fast and easy to receive it even from a satellite before receiving the actual blockchain – but they do ensure the correctness of the data.

6. *Storage machines.* These are the same to the state machines but they are vice versa in a matter of block size and organization: a block can be huge to store a binary data or it can be a reference for IPFS item, for example.

7. *Active content bridge.* It's responsible for making networks for DApps, calling a smart contract when the blockchain is producing an event to be handled – a token transfer, for example. It will call the active container JSON-RPC endpoint, so it can be even load balanced for a big amounts of smart contracts and DApps, like for an exchange – but the load balancing is done on OS kernel level, so you have no problem not just plugging it in, but also adding and removing units – it will be handled automatically. The architecture of the processing unit is totally unrelated, because smart contracts and DApps are published in pure source code on PHP7, so there is insurance, that it will be correctly interpreted and executed on any platform. A classical incoming endpoint is here as well, so as the bitcoin protocol in it – so almost all currently running integrations will have just one line replaced in their configuration files to utilize the HyperSphere.

And now we will take a deeper look at the blockvortex structure. It is a 3D structure, so let us work in a euclidean 3D coordinate system. As we will be talking about a step-up, we will have a strict increment on the Z-axis by one, as we will speak about a rotation – it's in a clockwise direction. Any vector is starting from one block and if it touches another block it means that it's checksum is placed at the corresponding place in a block description structure, but if it's not about the checksum – it means that it's one thread of blocks. A thread of blocks is a structure like the bitcoin blockchain – one connected to the previous one. Threads can be started and ended, they are natural numbers, if a thread is ended – it's number is the biggest one and it becomes vacant.

At point (0,0,0) there is a genesis block with all the initial data to fire up the system. Step up. We have four threads, and they can not be ended, so we do have at least four threads in the structure, not less. All of them do have the genesis block as a parent0. The block structure is a bit different due to the different structure of the blockvortex. We have the corresponding mandatory block fields, in order of data:
- *flag byte* – all eight bits are boolean flags
- *parent0* – a hash of the first parent. It can be null only if it's a genesis block, i.e. Z=0
- *parent1* – a hash of the second parent, if there's any. If there's not – get parent1 hash request returns null and there's null by default in a code representation of the structure.
- *height* – a Z coordinate of the block
- *thread number* – a number of thread this block belongs to

Each thread has a vacant slot – a place for a next block to be inserted, blocks are inserted from thread 1 to 2,3,4,e.t.c… An important notice – the block is finalized by its contents, so the mining task is getting easier, because the block structure will be predictable and unchanged, so you can pre-calculate Merkle tree's for them. After that blocks are got mined by PoW, and then signed by the elected masternodes with PoS locks and it finalizes the block in a thread. After that we're making a rotation and stepping up: so thread 1 will have *parent0* with a hash of a previous block for a thread consistency, and for *parent1* it will have a hash of a block on this place but one level below. So let us have NumThreads parameter as the current number of threads in a system – its a 4 or greater, natural number.

Each thread is mined separately at the same time by a group of the nodes who has indicated that they can mine, it's chosen by a Paxos algorithm for a computable number of blocks, other nodes are participating as a PoW validators(except masternodes), the masternodes are the learners in a Paxos algorithm because they are recording the data into the blockvortex registry. That eliminates the need in a mining pool at all – it's like a NiceHash or similar service built-in into the system: if you want to mine – just keep your device online, you will be elected, and when you're not mining – you still get the reward – see down strings.

Re-inventing the mining requires us to change a mining reward distribution. The reward consists of:
- _A new block reward_ – if there's any. The hard cap for a maximum coin supply can be increased by the network voting, but never decreased to prevent any kind of inconsistency or coin burning.
- _Fees from transactions in a block_. Zero cost transactions are prohibited, so even after a hard cap will be mined, mining will be ensured to stay profitable

After this step, we do have an amount of reward per block. It is coming to:
- _Miners group reward_. 45 %. A reward that is distributed across the miners that were elected to mine this block.
- _Masternodes reward_. 45 %. A reward that is distributed across the elected masternodes to sign and confirm the block. This reward is going 90% to the masternodes that are signing the block in blockvortex and 10% to the masternodes that were deploying it into MemDB.
- _Validators reward_. 5 %. First NumValidators confirmations of PoW correctness are rewarded to the nodes responded
- _Airdrop_. 4 %. A small part of each block reward is distributed across the nodes that we do see online, so it is a profitable case to just keep your node on
- _HyperSphere foundation_. 1 %. A small part is coming to the DAO that governs the system development and activities for ones who're pushing the project forward in its team.

To prevent ASIC's to break the game and perform the attacks, we're using multiple hashing algorithms rotated and tuned up with their internal parameters each time the difficulty is recalculated. So you can use your CPU and GPU to mine and perform all the checks required, but ASICs are technically impossible here due to the constant change of the hashing function. ASICs are not evil, but for our purpose we are avoiding them to address at least one important question that is standing now – a quantum supremacy. In the future we can safely add or remove some hashing functions if we will need it, but in ASIC it's technically impossible.

And here is the auto-scaling: let N be a NumThreads and the minimal value for the turns is N, so we can check if the $X=\dfrac{N^3+1}{N^2+N}$ rounded up is greater than N so we choose the greater one. Then we can analyze MemDB dynamics and make a decision – add or remove a thread. To make such a decision we're calculating a transactions per turn(TPT), transactions per minute(TPM) and we're writing it into a performance state machine as a numbers. After that we do calculate a depth parameter for the performance state machine which is the greater one of $\dfrac{N}{2}$ and a 2 – we will use it as a comparison depth for determining do we need to add or to remove a thread:

- if the TPT is going down and TPM is going down – we need to end a thread, there're too many threads and they're delaying the system
- if TPT is going up and TPM is going down – we need to add a thread to facilitate the increased load
- if TPT is going up but TPM is going up – we're OK
- if TPT is going down and TPM is going up – the difficulty must be revised to increase the protection of the system

If we're adding a thread, then it is inserted after the last one, new thread's first block parent0 will be the vector from the last thread's block, parent1 will be null. If we're removing a thread, then the last threads' new block parent1 will consume a vector from the last block of the removed thread. After adding or removing a thread we have to wait $\dfrac{N^2}{N+T}$ turns to let the system balance itself, T is a difference between TPT before and an iteration before the adjustment.

Once in a turn(one turn is when thread 1 is back to its original position [1,0, X]) - and making a turn state machine update, putting all the blocks in the turn position with their numbers, current NumThreads and Z value into a block in a turn-state machine thread and we're mining it with PoW/PoS as well, and once in a $\dfrac{N^5}{N^3+N+1}$ to a NumThreads we're updating a checkpoint state machine by archiving Z, turn state machine block number and it's hash in this machine's thread. It's mined as well. So if we do need to make sync of a node – we're getting a state machines chains first – it's a very fast and lightweight operation, and further we can safely start querying a neighbor nodes – no data forging will be possible because of the hashes preserved in a state machines.

Additional note to the node rewards: if somebody is willing to help a consensus and maintain a full copy of the blockchain – it will be rewarded automatically also for answering a get block questions.

So what can be announced in the system:
- ***Tokens***. As usual, event hook API for a standard events, announced with a smart contract handling it, with versioning support. A smart contract can be marked as completely immutable – no source code modifications or library version changes for the external libraries used, it can be marked as core-immutable – only libraries used can be switched to the new version through voting, or volatile contracts that can be modified in full. All modifications are voted. A token can be announced as in the main chain, so inside a subchain as well – it's a 1-to-1 process, just a receiving party API is a bit different.
- ***Smart contract alike DApps***, that can be also executed in Active containers, in source code. An open code will open not just an ability to make it truly portable, but also will open all the opportunities for code auditing and will eliminate the problem of "I'm not quite clear what I'm investing into".
- ***Libraries***, with versioning support for a further updates. Duplicating code is at least a non-productive tactics, so we need to provide a clear and straightforward way to publish, include and update the libraries.
- ***Desktop DApps*** in source code, with versioning support for a further updates. It is an illusion that PHP apps can make only a HTML pages! Actually, they can do whatever you wish even inside your desktop environment. And from recent times – it is OK to write a headless multi-threaded application on PHP. Times are changing, so should we.

- ***Separate chains*** – a tool called GBDL = Genesis Block Definition Language – is used to describe a new structure in a system, so it can be addressed from smart contracts and apps and also a Paxos mining search and data storage can be provided for such a structure. Provided services are paid in our token, not in the new chain's one. The announcement is stored inside a blockvortex, so to use it you need to configure your node with an object ID to join it, no code recompilation needed. This chain can have almost all the functionality as the main blockvortex: you can not announce a separate chain inside it to prevent the recursion.
- ***Bid/Ask requests for token exchange.*** Tokens are addressed in notation tokenID+objectID, so cross-subchain trading is automated and we do have one single true decentralized exchange. It has never been a purpose, but it's a mechanism for everyone to be able to offer "what I have" and ask for "what I want". There are no intermediates should be involved: neither centralized exchanges nor anything – it's an offer and a bid on it. As the tokens offered are locked for a time of the offer on the seller's account – all we need is a buyer who will propose a trade, so the system will match two requests automatically and in a decentralized manner. A remark about any kind of offline regulation – like the time showing us now, it's useless to try to forcibly implement in on a blockchain, it must be handled by the parties responsible: after all, taxes a paid to the governments to make some works done by them, not by owners of exchanges or a websites.
- ***Public keys***. The keys used for data signing, SSL/HTTPS and authenticity check. It gives us the ability to have a truly decentralized key verification service.
- ***Domains***. Network domains can be used to replace an obsolete and hierarchical structure we have now.

MemDB workflow cycle

A memdb is a tool to solve two big problems of modern blockchains:
- At the times of 51% attack or similar ones the end goal is to inject a fraud portion of transactions into the system. You can not do it in one block – because of the sanity checks, and you can not do it in a legitimate chain – it will be rejected. So the point is to flood the mempool and/or inject a pre-mined chain with malicious data like double-spending.
- If everything is OK, we do need to handle transaction spikes as well as we need to remember the fact of the spike to make a weighted up decision to add a thread

The problem is that if we will apply a simple local solution like memcachedb – it will still lack a quorum confirmation and can be played with. Another side is to use a DPoS to do the job – it provides a block every 5 seconds – but it will kill any attempt of decentralization on its root. So the PoS mechanism benefit is used to make an offload block of the system. This transaction accumulator is facilitating multiple tasks that are making blockchain faster:
- *Block contents finalization*. If we're speaking about the PoW mining, there is no strict requirement to include all the transactions from mempool into the block mined, the greater work for a block – so here is the winner. In fact, even an empty block can be mined, so it opens a trapdoor to the empty blockchain attack: a malicious miner can safely ignore any mempool transaction and will just produce an empty block with greater work and they will actually be inserted into the blockchain. This case is technically impossible in our system because the blocks are fed into the MemDB from mempool and their contents are immutable since this moment. Because of MemDB serial nature, there can be no glitches about where to put the block – it is one thread of blocks.
- *Sanity checking*. Every transaction is checked by its digital signature first, but it's not enough to be sure that everything is valid. The most common cause is overspending, so we're checking

balances of the sending party. More complex transactions like smart contract deployment or sub-chain announce are also have their sanity checks. It saves a lot of time to the blockvortex if there are much fewer things to be checked.
- *Transaction backlog*. Yes, every hashing algorithm can be hacked or brute-forced, it's just a question of resources – so we must be prepared to defend the system in case of the hash power attack. And if we will have any need for any reason to re-construct the blockvortex – we do need an ability to look back at the transaction pool and maybe re-mine the blocks. So here it is.

MemDB has three tunable parameters:
- *Cursor*. It's a place in a thread where is the next block to be inserted into the blockvortex resides. When the block is inserted into the blockvortex – the cursor value is incremented.
- *Depth*. It is a standard backlog depth for MemDB, so the regular node can safely trim the blocks that are deeper from cursor than this positive integer value. It's not an obligation for a node to use the global value – a node can be configured to keep a deeper log, but not a smaller one. So if your node was configured to keep 128 blocks and the global depth parameter was tuned to become 130 – the node will select the greater value to be consistent in a network.
- *Quorum*. It's a minimal number of masternodes elected to maintain the PoS thread for MemDB. The masternodes are receiving the reward for this as well when the block is mined, but this reward is smaller than the block signing reward in a blockvortex. This value is safe to increase in time when the number of masternodes will rise.

A safety mechanism is to make a fallback for Quorum value to prevent the attack vector when we will have not enough masternodes to maintain a network to accept the blocks. If there will be no masternodes eligible and available – memdb will keep searching for a masternodes and the task will be delegated to the masternodes signing the blockvortex blocks.

Depth parameter is different for different types of masternodes because they can automatically propose system parameters tuning and to do the analysis they must keep the MemDB data to correlate it with performance state machine data for a load spike detection.

Masternode types

We do need some nodes to do the additional job for a system, so it was obvious that we are using masternodes for it. The deposit is locked in a single transaction, so its TXO is used when the masternode announces its presence in a network. The deposit amount must be exactly the amount of a masternode's role lock requirement, so all other nodes will check the balance of the wallet and will lock up this exact amount as a safety deposit. To make masternodes affordable for a regular users – the starting amount to be locked is 1000 tokens. Roles of the masternode are cumulative, so the next level of masternode is performing all the tasks of the previous one and additional tasks that are more sensitive for the system and because of that the reward is higher, so as the safety deposit.

- 1000 tokens → The basic masternode maintains a MemDB PoS thread for block reception. This task is simple and it is needed everywhere in a network, so it's a logical choice for every masternode.
- 2500 tokens → the masternode for a state machines block signing and for storage checking oracle
- 5000 tokens → the masternode for block signing when the blocks are inserted into blockvortex.
- 10000 tokens → the masternode for Paxos aid that acts as election moderator.

- 20000 tokens → the masternode for a blockvortex speed analysis that can propose thread removal
- 25000 tokens → the masternode for a blockvortex speed analysis that can propose thread creation
- 50000 tokens → the masternode for a system parameters analysis that can propose a vote for MemDB parameters change.

The first question from here is why the creation of a new thread is more important than removal? The answer is that we can easily check if we need to remove a thread just by a simple parameter analysis. It's mathematically easy to spot the situation when we actually don't need a thread that is slowing us down because of the too wide circle. But when to add a thread? It requires a deeper MemDB analysis and correlation with a performance state machine data – it can be a local spike that is gone, it will be handled and no further actions are needed. Also, we can look even deeper into the MemDB and performance state machine data to detect the regular spikes – like a business day start, so we can add an extra thread before the spike will actually occur and the users will notice the slowing down.

One extra reward for a non-regular node – a full node reward. A full node is maintaining a copy of blockvortex, state machines and MemDB that is deeper than required for a quorum. Yes, the hard drives are cheap now, but the data size can grow to a significant size, and there can be a need for the really old data. So the get block request is addressed to the full nodes through the network. And this request is tracked, so the requesting party is not paying for this – but it will be a reward for such a node from the system at the moment of airdrop.

Airdrop philosophy

Why do we use an airdrop every block? Or why do we use it at all? We could be distributing tokens on the start of the system and it would be enough for a start and further growth – actually, no. The problem that we are solving using airdrop is an availability problem.

Take a look at crypto coins and tokens generally – it's more than ten years of the ecosystem development – but why you don't see it everywhere? Integrated, used and applied. Where are all of them? The "availability" is a key in all it's meanings to explain why we do have the situation we have now.

It's unavailable to the end-user. Bitcoin and other major coins are relatively expensive, and mining has become a rare thing, so – it's not a central bank, but a small group of people can produce new coins. Either by PoW difficulty avalanche or by the PoS/DPoS centralized "buy it first" nature – the coin generation process is semi-centralized. In HyperSphere, we are eliminating the mining pools and giving every device a role by using the Paxos algorithm. And yes – even a router or an IoT device can be a validator of the PoW block and get a reward for that. It's an honest opportunity for everybody.

It's unavailable to the merchant. Wait a minute – bitcoin JSON-RPC protocol is a standard de facto nowadays, and all you need to do is to launch a node… Technically – yes, but the problem is that more than 75% is a service or a re-selling of real goods. With a service it's relatively easy: you are providing a service by yourself and you are the one who decides what to trade your service for. With real goods, it's harder, because we need to integrate the system first of all – at the very end of the chain: at the farm where the food is grown, at the lumber mill where the wood is handled et cetera… And at such a place we do often have a very bad network connection or even no connection at all. That's why we are starting with routers and network software – not just because of privacy, but also because of availability to the very persons and companies who can start the supply chain for a real trade. Only when the merchant and the regular consumer will be able to pay for food, electricity, and water with tokens – then the change will start.

Another problem here is logistics: fossil fuel production is monopolized by a small pack of corporations and no car will go without a gas – until now: electric cars and trucks are the keys to change the game. Fossil fuels are unavailable for adopting new technologies not because the technology does not fit their need – on a contrary, it fits their tasks very well, the reason is that these corporations are controlled by the people and governments who do not want to make a change that will enable people to be more independent. As California showed us by its time-proven example – everybody can produce electricity easily, with excess and without any harm caused to nature. So the grid networks can help to exchange the electricity on a peer to peer basis, and using crypto coins is the easiest way to make mutual settlements. Grid power networks are our far goal of integration, this will be a project to literally power everybody up.

It's unavailable to trade for old resources. Looking at authorities fighting the crypto projects we must notice, that a lot of fraud and scum ones are prosecuted as it should be and it's a good thing: our taxes are prepayment for peacekeeping services from the state… But take a look who else got hit most of the times? Without any real grounds to be prosecuted? Exchanges and trading platforms, crypto bank cards. Volatile nature of the crypto is not an argument at all after a Great Depression in the USA and Tulip Fever in the Netherlands and many other market crush events – everything is volatile, that's the fact. Why the places and services that are doing a great job – are the primary target? As I've mentioned up strings, crypto coins and tokens are very easy to integrate into the merchant work cycle – so what if the people will exchange fiat money to coins with ease and will pay with it in a store, online and send to each other? Fiat money will show their primary purpose in months – they are made to rob people, and the crypto-coin transactions will eliminate an army of a middle man and will fuel up the regular people. In time people will just stop converting their crypto back to the fiat money because the crypto coins will become a usual part of their lives. Because of that, any place or service that makes a bridge is hit and made inconvenient for a people – most of them do not have patience and won't use things that are not convenient. That's why we are eliminating the need for the single place that can be taken down – a global exchange for everything is built on a truly decentralized network, no single point of failure here.

And – actually – an airdrop was already tested in the offline world as an unconditional basic income. This idea was fitting for testing, but it could not be for a long because of its immaturity. However, the root of the idea is brilliant: we are giving people a small number of satoshis to use the system. If the person wants to earn more – it can participate in the network more actively. So the coins are available by fact to all the users of the network – and the useful services can be utilized using them.

Why other people will provide their goods and services for our coins? Because even on a start phase they are backed by the need of transferring data and keeping the security and privacy intact. As the integrations will be added – more real-world cases will be tightly connected with the coin and it will increase the demand for it.

State machines

We're using state machines to provide a robust and parallel state propagation for a different system parameters, here are the main ones:
- *Checkpoint state machine* – it is used to have a quick notebook of the blockvortex that can be propagated on literally any channel in a simplex mode because of the hashing block chain

thread scheme. No, it was not specially tailored to be broadcasted from some particular source, but the ability to make a fast tamper-protecting protection without a full quorum is a handy one. A basic steps towards it were taken when the bitcoin blockchain was broadcasted over the middle range air, so the node that was supposed to e autonomous was able to pick it up – but the main mistake there was a the matter transferred: Bitcoin blockchain is some kind of heavy for open-air broadcasts. And as the code update will be in order – we can safely incorporate this data into the code and have a stable and lightweight block database.

- *Performance state machine* – it is used to store the metrics of the blockchain and to determine do we need to add or remove threads. The basic math behind the calculations is selected after many experiments with a many more complex ones. But speaking forward – will you be pleased if you'll have your wristwatch battery go down or experience a heat burn just because your smartwatch was calculating a very complex problem for a greater good?
- *Turn state machine* - it is taking part in maturing not a single blocks, but a whole turns – it's a more detailed version of the checkpoint state machine and it's synchronized right after it, so no forged blocks will be inserted. This line of defense looks an overwhelming from a first glance, but if we will take a deeper look at the 51% attack vectors – the necessity of this state machine is unquestionable: it provides a really fast and accountable interface to make a blocks hashes sealed in one more way so the attacks are much more difficult to perform.
- *Blob storage state machine* – it's an IPFS-to-blockchain registry that describes the data that we can get from the global CDN-like network. The purpose of this machine is to propagate a route for both big data and the small pieces – without a block system abuse or overload. The simplest representation for this machine is an announcement engine for a web browser cache for static content that was already signed: like jQuery scripts. Whatever the website's logic is – it can not alter *the original code* of the framework, so it has to be loaded *intact as it is*. And if you're able to do so really fast – you will be safe even if you have reinstalled your device or a virtual machine from a scratch.
- *Certificate authority state machine* – it provides storage for keys and certificates, so you can always grab root keys for PKI and a single key for a signature.
- *System state machine* – a meta-machine that is running only if it's selected to be and it can be running on a full node only. It provides a system state changes in a form of balances among the addresses through time. It helps to analyze the system deeper and to speed up the fintech and DeFi related services.
- *DNS machine* – it provides a truly decentralized DNS infrastructure along with the certificate authority state machine for DNSSEC keys.

It's a good question – why? We do have a network consensus and a quorum so why do we need anything else? The answer is in the real world: we do have censorship and a mangling of the data to silence some things up. The problem is – and what we are doing now for – is to put the wrong things right. UHF, SW and other things are very useful to transmit small but significant portions of the data. So if the full blockvortex synchronization is not possible – at least a checkpoints can be picked up like even from a satellite.

Governance and Voting

Nothing can be defined perfectly from the very first time, and even if it was – it has to have an ability to adapt to the changes and the time. So we do have not just opaque parameters of a blockvortex like a NumThreads, but we do have volatile ones as well. It's OK if we can take a look at the past and make our mathematical rules more fitting the real world. So these are the basic ones that we need to be able to change:

- *Total token supply*. It can be incremented with a magnitude vote. Look at the Bitcoin now – it's too expensive to be purchased by a regular person. Regardless of the time if a blockchain pizza
- *Thread re-evaluation time*. It is balanced by the math, but sometimes we can apply a more complex algorithms to analyze the long way of running to propose a change for a better good
- *Improvement proposals implementation*. Yes, it will not be a directive, but it will show a good priority scheduling for a feature list
- *Smart contract parameters*. If it is allowed by conditions of the contract announcement, a change will serve for a better good to all it's users if it's accepted by the magnitude of the adopters. The typical case is the revenue sharing contracts.
- *Subchain parameters*. Yes, they can be tweaked also – so as the main vortex ones, and it serves the same purpose.

A voting mechanism is not just a yes or no dialog – to vote for or against something you are required to lock your tokens for your vote for an amount of time. If your vote is not winning – your tokens will be released at half of the length. If your vote has won the election – your tokens will be locked for a full time. The longer you're locking your tokens – the greater the weight is in case of the same amount of time: $W = \dfrac{N^2 + T^3}{N + T + 1}$ where W is the weight, N is the amount of tokens locked and T is a number of turns. This mechanism is successfully preventing us from a fat cat problem when the person can buy a lot of tokens or rise a lot of nodes to mangle the vote – the tokens are about to be locked for a long time, so you will be responsible for your vote whatever the outcome will be. When the proposal for a vote is propagated, it has its criteria for a percent of the nodes voted, percent of the stake voted, minimal locking time and minimal locking stake – so the flood voting can be efficiently filtered off in conjunction with sanity checking for a votes:
- at least 75% of votes collected must vote for some option
- at least 75% of stake must be voting
- locking time is not less than a 10000 turns

Descriptor problem

The key blocker in many projects before this one was the approach: it was multiple attempts to just install the software for mesh networks, blockchain, darknets – and trying just to tweak the configuration of each one up. The problem is that it has caused an incrementing lag avalanche that was breaking the system. The solution is not so straightforward but it's the only one – we have to use a single descriptors pool for every component. That's how it can be implemented:
- *The blockchain* – directly and indirectly through the state machines it is used as a distributed database where you can make a query for a public key. The one to rule them all – mesh, Tor, I2P e.t.c.
- *The mesh* – it provides the OSI L2 segment maintenance and it is its sole task. All the descriptors are taken from the descriptor handling daemon. OSI Layer 3 addresses are derived from the public key.
- *The darknet* – it is used when an end-user especially needs that kind of privacy. The privacy is always a trade-off, so a simple TCPCrypt that is a time-proven solution is more than enough and the only reason for doing the encryption is a nature of a mesh networks – they're forwarding packets by the shortest path, the encryption is totally not their problem to solve: they're giving you a full OSI Layer 2. And the overlays like Yggdrasil are making things more

convenient to use providing us an IP addresses/subnets derived from a public key – so the regular software will have an ability to just bind to IP address without any further code changes.

The root of the problem is that every software piece is trying and establishing it's very own and private keyspace. At the first look - it's OK, because if it is *alone in the dark* – it is the only thing an app can do. But if you're about to use at least two applications together – why don't they both have an endpoint to bind to the "key master" program, hello The Matrix? An algorithms are quite standardizable, especially if the common frameworks like OpenSSL are used, so the key lengths are still the same integer numbers… The problem is not in the fact that every privacy-oriented package is trying to survive on its own when it is – the problem is that it was not even an idea that they can work together. Actually – they should.

Certificate and key management

As for every cryptography-related project with keys – we must have a key management routines. But we have a way bigger solution – a new way of working with keys. Key management is necessary on the main network frontiers:
- *DNS*. Yes, we do have a centralized system that is unreliable by its workflow and it's under full control of a small group of people.
- *SSL/HTTPS*. Certificates are signed by a centralized authorities and can be revoked by them at will – actually, why?
- *PGP* and other signatures – we need to have a way to pass our key safely, just like in a personal meeting.

For DNS there are two problems in one. First of all, it's hierarchical and on any branch from the root servers to the end user's server there can be a silent intrusion. As we do have now a distributed data storage using blockchain technology – why do we need this centralized storage at all? It's much easier and secure to put the data into the digitally signed distributed storage and get data from there. It's secure, because you can be sure not just about the data authenticity, but if you are using the full node your request will be done and handled locally from your copy of the block data, so no data leak over the network. A second problem is a DNSSEC key, but it does not exist in a blockchain because it's already signed by the key which has announced the domain – the real owner's key.

SSL and HTTPS are relying on the asymmetric cryptography to provide authenticity, so we're looking at the wider task we need to solve – we must provide a full solution for a Public Key Infrastructure workflow. It's simple – thanks to the blockchain architecture:
- The certificate can be signed by itself to start a PKI and published in a blockchain. X.509 standard has all the headers and options required to determine that it's a Certificate Agency(CA) root item or it's a certificate signed by CA or itself. Since the certificate is placed inside a blockchain – we can have a TXO that is unique and we can use it to address any further operations with a certificate.
- The revocation can be signed by the certificate's Private key or by the Certificate Agency – it depends on the settings for the CA and a certificate. As the certificate was revoked – it's a public part is removed from the storage on all the nodes except the full ones.
- Certificate request can be sent through a blockchain – because it's a public key and the information fields you're sending and it is already signed by the transaction author – no data modification is possible.

- CRL = Certificate Revocation List – This feature is a bit obsolete but still in use at some places. This is a stateless query to the block data for a pre-defined period, it can be done on a local node.
- OCSP = Online Certificate Status Protocol – this request can be served locally also, but this is one of the most important parts: TLS and HTTPS are relying on it for security checking, but if the OCSP responder is down – it is silently ignored. The ignoring part is fine because in another scenario all the TLS connections would stale if no responder is working. But in almost any privacy intrusion attack OCSP is jammed. This will be a weak spot no more.

And – speaking of keys we can not miss the upgrade opportunity for blockchain keys: we are introducing a key family term. As we will take a look, a wallet.dat file is a private key, so – why don't we sign by our main key that we're keeping in a secure place our keys for a smartwatch, mobile wallet, desktop PC wallet? Nothing prevents us from doing so – we can generate a key and announce it on the network – and then just use it as a wallet.dat in the device, keeping the main key secured in cold storage. A useful outcome for it is an ability to indicate a multi-spend ability, so this key will be able to spend the funds from the slave ones and see their balances. It is implemented as follows:

1. We generate a master key – our wallet.dat, as usual.
2. We generate a slave wallet2.dat on the same wallet, signing public key for wallet2.dat with our master key from step 1
3. We are running the slave wallet with wallet2.dat, synchronizing it and in case of demand from wallet.dat, the amount demanded will be transferred to its address.

Also, key families are securing the masternodes from a key theft – even if a slave private key is stolen – it can not spend the amount locked and it can be revoked. Yes, a reward can be stolen if it was stored on the slave address, but the main deposit is intact. Also issuing a slave key for a masternode can specify a different reward address if desired – it is another level of protection.

Ecosystem

As you can see now the functional blocks of the core platform, we're about to make it more useful for real problems of the user, here is the list of things coming to production-grade first:

- A truly decentralized ***messenger***, with p2p instant messaging, voice and video streams
- ***Decentralized email*** – you will receive your messages to your nodes directly, so no PRISM on a mail servers (hello, Yahoo!)
- ***Certificate handling infrastructure*** to verify SSL, digital signatures, PGP and PKI
- Decentralized DNS with a transparent decentralized mechanism of DNSSEC key announcement
- ***Storage subsystem***. So you can achieve the true conception of CDN. Torrents here are also "a must" - it's a very good mechanism that was mangled to a chimera we do have now for the sake of centralization and control
- ***Virtual Networks***. You will be able to rise not just a VPN-like service to access the internet, but also to maintain your truly private network like for your company branch offices – and all of this without a single point of failure
- ***DApps*** with a fully-featured decentralized app marked. It's open-source, it uses our core token, and it can not be banned, jammed or mangled in other ways modern markets do nowadays. All the application signatures are yours, so no market stripping and signing by their key like in Microsoft Store – you can be 100% ensured that the user will receive your very own application without any modifications.
- ***Decentralized governance***: propose your polls, vote for one of the variants or value of a parameter, look at your vote anytime to be sure that it was not messed with.

Roadmap

Now it's time to implement a stable release and integrate it into solving real-world problems that are related to regular people – we don't care about any kind of political or regulatory artificial macro-problems made by a small group of people who're thinking that they are masters of the world. The stages are following:

1. The initial release of the pre-built routers and devices for different use cases: mobile pocket and car routers, stationary home and SOHO routers, smartwatch and mobile applications. This will be done via the Kickstarter campaign at Nov-Dec 2019, delivery starting at the beginning of 2020 like in February – it depends on the amount of devices pre-purchased and the logistics. System functionality will be mostly network-related and the blockchain will be launched in a very basic but debugged and production-ready form.
2. Router production will continue, and so the development. We will make a hardware line expansion and will launch the smart contracts at the beginning of April-2020.
3. At the June-2020 we're about to add the DApps and at the same time it's a big expansion for the package list, so the Linux OS distribution will have a full desktop functionality
4. For August-2020 we will release a stable Android build from a scratch, based on AOSP(Android Open Source Project)

Any further development and integration process is unpredictable now because of too many factors involved and the results of these four steps we do not know now.